S0-BEC-813

For my husband, Chris, and our sons,
Christopher, Beau, and Dylan. The four of you
have supported me so much on this journey. You
have been my cheerleaders and taste testers.
Most importantly, you did it with me.

Published by Familius LLC, www.familius.com

Familius books are available at special discounts for bulk purchases, whether
for sales promotions or for family or corporate use. For more information,
contact Familius Sales at 559-876-2170 or email orders@familius.com.
Reproduction of this book in any manner, in whole or in part, without written
permission of the publisher is prohibited.

Library of Congress Cataloging-in-Publication Data
2018956197
Paperback ISBN 9781641701082
Ebook ISBN 9781641701389

Printed in China

Edited by Lacey Wulf
Cover design by David Miles
Book design by David Miles and Brooke Jorden
Photography by Todd Stone

10 9 8 7 6 5 4 3 2

First Edition

LARA LYN CARTER

SKINNY
SOUTHERN

90 REINVENTED CLASSICS WITHOUT THE GUILT!

FAMILIUS

CONTENTS

BECOMING A SKINNY SOUTHERNER

I t happens to all of us sooner or later. There is "that birthday" looming on the horizon that makes you stop and think. For some it is forty, for others fifty, but for me it was forty-seven. It was three months before my forty-seventh birthday when I decided to make a lifestyle change. I had to get back into shape and lose weight after having a baby at almost forty-three years old, but how do I avoid food when my life revolves around it?

I am a private chef, Emmy award–winning television host of *Thyme for Sharing*, cookbook author of *Southern Thymes Shared*, and founder of Wicker & Whisk—a gourmet line of clean-eating sauces. My life literally is all about food. In addition, I am a wife and a mother of three boys, ages twenty-two, sixteen, and five. Yes, five!

Food is just as big a part of my family life as it is my professional life. No one in the family was going to be happy if I cooked boring food. So, I made the decision that I was going to create delicious meals, just as I always had, but healthier and cleaner. No boring baked chicken and plain salads were going to dare grace my Southern table. Southern food is comfort food! People expect dishes like fried chicken, cornbread, fried green tomatoes, pound cakes, and, of course, grits. Traditionally a lot of Southern foods are fried and often breaded with flour, which has gluten. How could I get the traditional flavor that people love but present it in a clean way?

As a chef, I knew that I would have to push my culinary skills to keep my family and myself happy while trying to be healthier. The thought of being bored with cooking, when it is what I love so dearly, was terrifying. I had to learn to avoid processed foods, gluten, and refined sugar; limit dairy; and add more plant-based foods to replace dairy. For the first 120 days of my lifestyle change, I created a new recipe every day, putting my creativity to the test.

I also made a commitment that I would faithfully work out, incorporating weight training and cardio. Exercising in itself was a challenge in the beginning. I have always told people: "If you see me running, call the police because someone is chasing me!" Exercise was something I did half-heartedly in the past, but now it is a regular part of my life. I actually love working out. I have discovered muscles and strength I never knew I had.

I lost 46 pounds and went from a size 12 to a size 2. What began as something that I thought I would suffer through to reach my goals of becoming healthy and fit has become a new passion. I found that it was actually possible to lose the weight from having a late-in-life baby. And what's more, I found that you can eat healthy without sacrificing flavor.

Cooking has been the biggest blessing. My creativity is challenged every day, and I love it! I haven't given up anything. I have simply added a new culinary passion—glorious food that is delicious, beautiful, healthy, and clean!

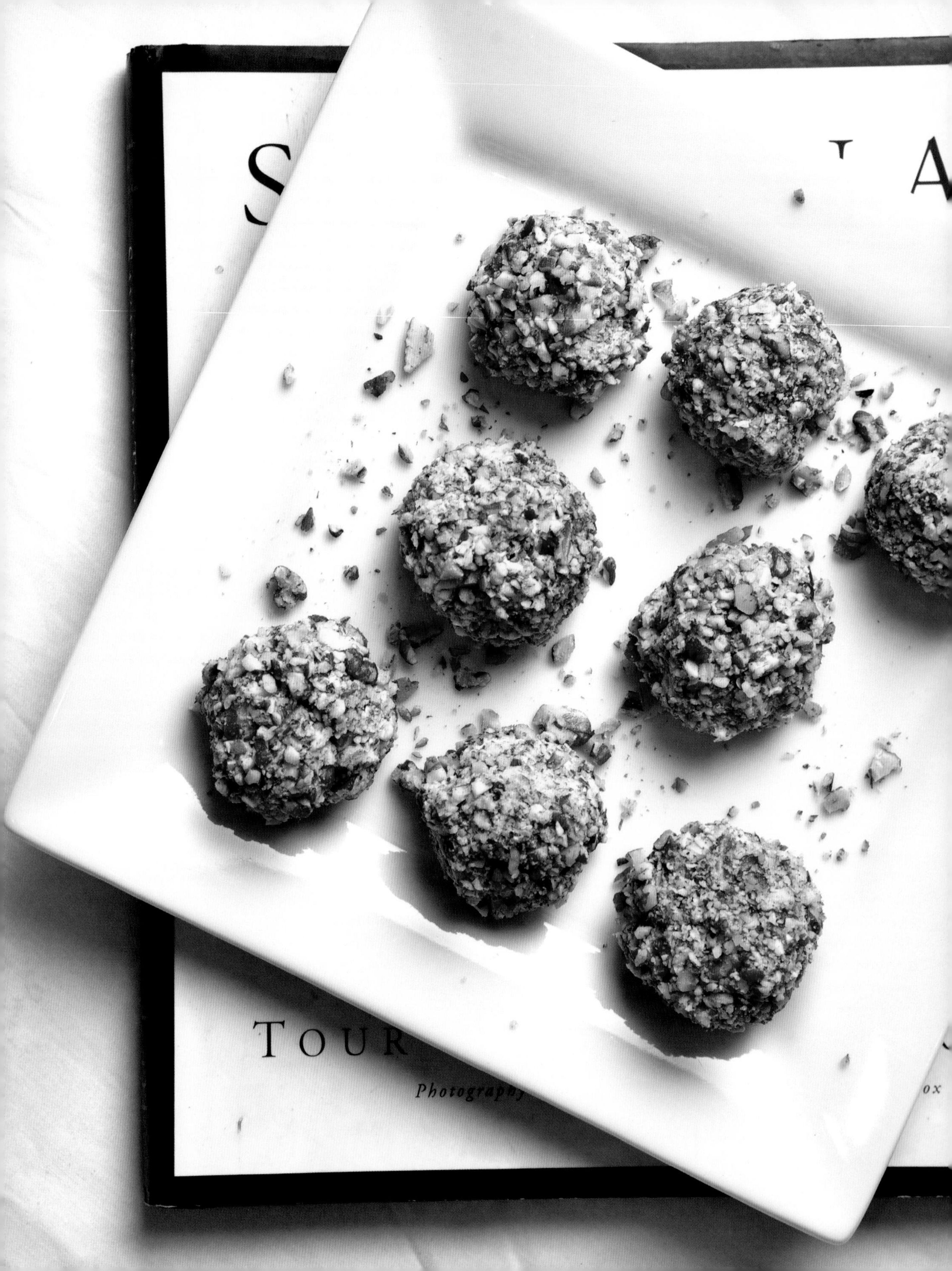
Photography

CHAPTER 1

APPETIZERS

CHIPOTLE MAPLE PECANS

These are a delicious combination of sweet and spicy. Not only are they perfect for parties, but they are also a great addition to a tailgate!

SERVES 12

2 EGG WHITES

1/4 CUP PURE MAPLE SYRUP

1 1/2 TEASPOONS CINNAMON

1/2 TEASPOON CUMIN

1/4 TEASPOON CHIPOTLE POWDER

1 POUND FRESH PECAN HALVES

1 Preheat the oven to 325 degrees.

2 In a large bowl, whip the egg whites with the syrup, cinnamon, cumin, and chipotle powder.

3 Add the pecans and stir them well into the egg white mixture.

4 Place the pecans on a parchment-lined baking sheet and spread them evenly so that they are all flat. Bake the pecans for 10 minutes.

5 Remove the pecans from the oven and stir them again. Return the pecans to the oven for 10 more minutes.

6 Allow the pecans to cool completely and store in an airtight container.

CINNAMON AND SPICE CHICKEN WINGS

For this football mom, tailgating is a very big deal. This wing recipe will be a touchdown for your team!

SERVES 6

2 TABLESPOONS OLIVE OIL

2 CLOVES OF GARLIC, MINCED

1/2 CUP DICED SWEET ONION

1 TABLESPOON SALT

4 TABLESPOONS HONEY

1/2 TEASPOON GROUND CINNAMON

4 TABLESPOONS TOMATO PASTE

ZEST AND JUICE OF 1 LIME

2 1/2 POUNDS CHICKEN WINGS, TIPS REMOVED

1   Preheat the oven to 400 degrees.

2   In a skillet, sauté the garlic and onion in olive oil over medium heat for 2 minutes. Add the salt, honey, cinnamon, and tomato paste, stirring well.

3   Remove the skillet from the heat and stir in the lime zest and juice. Allow the mixture to cool.

4   Divide the sauce in half. Place the wings in a large plastic bag. Pour half of the sauce over the wings. Marinate the wings for 6–8 hours or overnight. Reserve the remainder of the sauce for cooking the wings.

5   Remove the wings from the marinade and arrange them on a greased baking sheet. Place the wings in the oven for 15 minutes.

6   Warm the remaining sauce slightly. Remove the wings from the oven, drizzle them with the remaining sauce and stir them to coat well.

7   Return the wings to the oven for an additional 15 minutes and serve.

CRAB DIP

Summers spent on the Gulf Coast and all of the delicious fresh seafood that goes with it are the inspiration for this dip.

SERVES 12

2 CUPS CHOPPED VIDALIA ONION (OR ANY SWEET ONION)

1/2 CUP CHOPPED RED PEPPER

1/2 CUP CHOPPED GREEN PEPPER

1/2 CUP GRATED SWISS CHEESE

1 CUP OLIVE OIL MAYONNAISE

1 CUP ALMOND-BASED CREAM CHEESE

1 POUND LUMP CRABMEAT

1 TABLESPOON FRESH LIME JUICE

1 Preheat the oven to 350 degrees.

2 Mix all the ingredients together and pour into a baking dish that has been sprayed with cooking spray.

3 Bake for 35 to 40 minutes, and serve warm.

FRICAS

I love this classic appetizer. Adding fresh rosemary gives it beautiful color and flavor.

SERVES 8

8 OUNCES PARMESAN CHEESE, GRATED   2 TABLESPOONS DRIED ROSEMARY

1   Preheat the oven to 400 degrees.

2   On a parchment-lined baking sheet, pour the cheese one tablespoon at a time, making sure to leave room for spreading.

3   Sprinkle rosemary evenly over the cheese. Place the pan in the oven for 8–10 minutes.

4   Cool the fricas completely before removing them from the parchment and serving.

HERB DIP

Perfect as a dip for crudité and gluten-free crackers, this recipe can also pull double duty as a spread for lettuce wraps!

◇◇

SERVES 10

1/2 CUP OLIVE OIL MAYONNAISE

1/2 CUP ALMOND-BASED CREAM CHEESE

1 TEASPOON ROSEMARY

1 TABLESPOON CHOPPED FRESH BASIL

PINCH OF SALT AND PEPPER

1 CLOVE OF GARLIC, MINCED

2 TABLESPOONS LEMON JUICE

1   Mix all ingredients and serve with crudité or pita chips. This is excellent on grilled mushrooms!

OLIVE PECAN DIP

The cayenne pepper packs a little pop of heat. This dip is also delicious served warm on top of chicken!

SERVES 12

6 OUNCES GREEN OLIVES, SLICED

1/2 CUP FINELY CHOPPED PECANS

1 TABLESPOON MINCED GARLIC

1/4 TEASPOON CAYENNE PEPPER, OR TO TASTE

5 TABLESPOONS PECAN OIL

1   Mix all ingredients together and chill for 30 minutes to allow the pecans to soften.

2   Place the mixture into a food processor or blender and pulse 5-6 times and serve.

SAVORY PECAN TRUFFLES

People usually think of truffles as sweet. My savory version is a two bite–size ball of creamy and crunchy, complimented by pecan truffle oil.

SERVES 8

14 OUNCES PLANT-BASED CREAM CHEESE

2 TABLESPOONS MINCED FRESH CHIVES

1 TABLESPOON PECAN TRUFFLE OIL

1 TABLESPOON MINCED GARLIC

1/2 TEASPOON COARSE GROUND BLACK PEPPER

1/4 TEASPOON COARSE SALT

1 CUP CHOPPED PECANS

1   Except the pecans, combine all ingredients together well. Cover the mixture and place it in the refrigerator for 30 minutes.

2   Pour the pecans in a bowl. Divide the mixture evenly into 14 truffles and roll them in the pecans to coat them evenly.

3   Place the truffles in the refrigerator for 30 more minutes or until ready to serve.

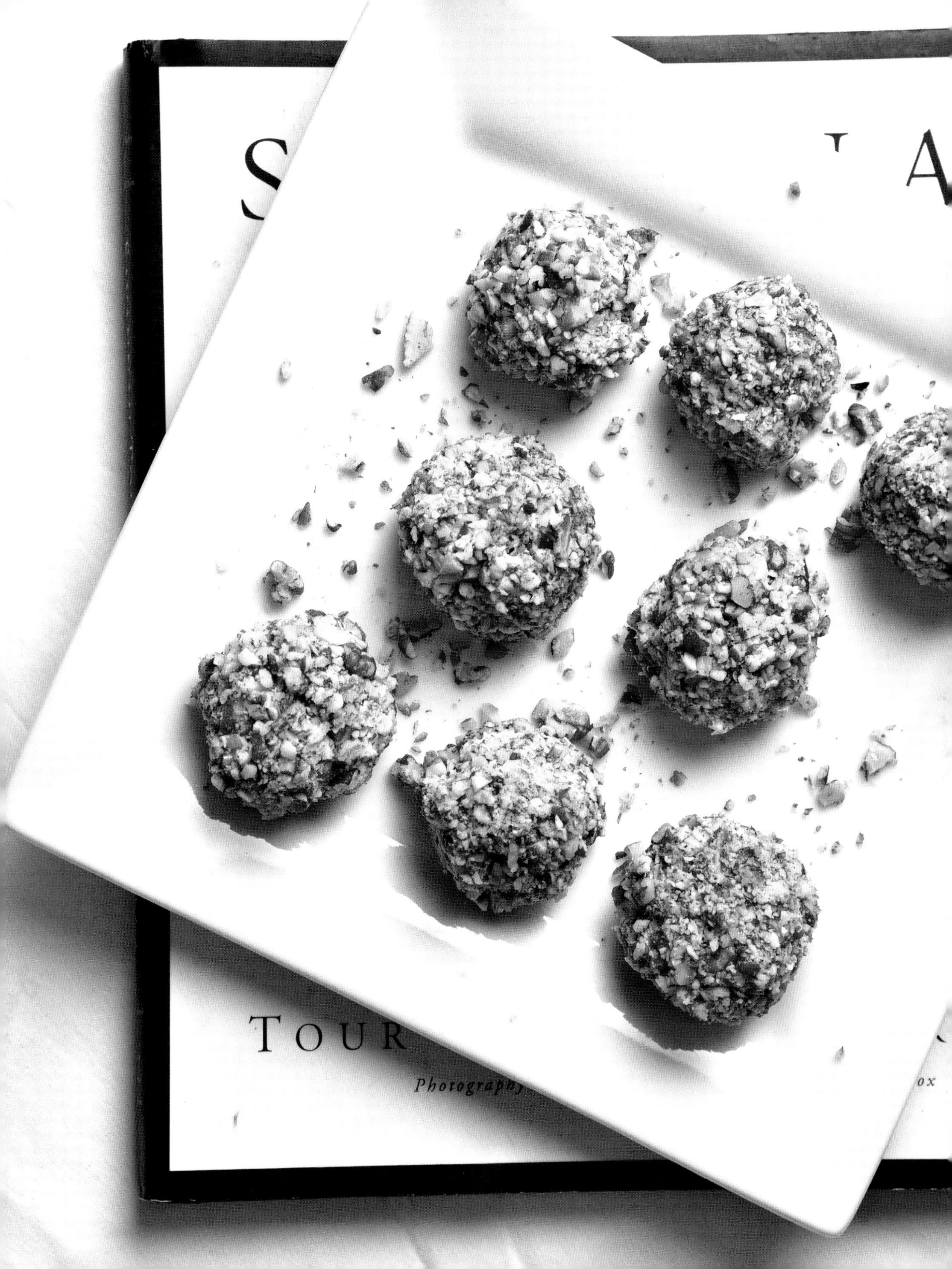
TOUR
Photography

SPICY BOILED PEANUTS

Hold everything! A tailgate is not complete without boiled peanuts, and these are really worth raving over!

SERVES 18

3 POUNDS GREEN BOILING PEANUTS

3 LARGE LIMES

4 LARGE JALAPEÑO PEPPERS, CUT IN HALF

6 CLOVES OF GARLIC, PEELED

1 TABLESPOON CUMIN

1 TABLESPOON CELERY SALT

1 TABLESPOON ONION POWDER

1 TABLESPOON GARLIC POWDER

1 TABLESPOON PAPRIKA

6 TABLESPOONS CHILI POWDER

1 TEASPOON CAYENNE PEPPER

1/2 CUP COARSE SALT

1   Put the peanuts in a large stock pot and cover them with water.

2   Zest and juice the limes and add the zest, juice, and peel to the pot.

3   Add all the remaining ingredients. Bring the peanuts to a boil.

4   Reduce the heat to low and cook covered for 4 hours. Be sure to stir the peanuts every 30 minutes and add water as needed to keep peanuts covered.

5   After 4 hours, remove the pot from the heat and allow the contents to sit in the pot for 8 hours.

6   Drain the peanuts and remove the remains of the peppers, garlic, and limes. Rinse the peanuts and drain them well. Store the peanuts in the refrigerator until serving.

STUFFED PEPPERS

These little beauties pack a punch of flavor and color. The crisp peppers and creamy filling are light and refreshing.

8 OUNCES ALMOND-BASED CREAM CHEESE

8 OUNCES ROASTED RED PEPPERS, DRAINED

1 TEASPOON MINCED GARLIC

1 TEASPOON CHOPPED FRESH ROSEMARY

1 TABLESPOON CHOPPED FRESH BASIL

2 TABLESPOONS FRESH LEMON JUICE

1/2 TEASPOON COARSE SALT

1/2 TEASPOON COARSE GROUND BLACK PEPPER

10 MINI SWEET BELL PEPPERS

1   In a blender or food processor, combine all ingredients except the bell peppers. Mix for about 30 seconds to create a smooth consistency.

2   Wash the peppers and cut them in half. Remove the seeds from the peppers.

3   Divide the dip evenly among the peppers and chill in the refrigerator for 1 hour before serving.

TRUFFLE DEVILED EGGS

Every Southern lady has a deviled egg recipe. Mine has a twist from pecan truffle oil produced right down the road from my hometown!

SERVES 6

6 LARGE BOILED EGGS, CUT IN HALF

3 TABLESPOONS OLIVE OIL MAYONNAISE

1 TABLESPOON DIJON MUSTARD

2 TABLESPOONS PECAN TRUFFLE OIL

1 TEASPOON COARSE SALT

1/2 TEASPOON COARSE GROUND BLACK PEPPER

2 TABLESPOONS CHIVES, FINELY CHOPPED AND DIVIDED

1   Place the yolks from the eggs in a medium bowl. Add all the remaining ingredients except half of the chives and mix well.

2   Fill the egg whites evenly with the mixture and sprinkle with the remaining chives and serve.

CHAPTER 2

RUBS, SPICE BLENDS, AND SAUCES

BARBECUE SEASONING RUB

Spicy or sweet? I say, "Both!" This rub is the perfect blend, and great for chicken, pork, or even brisket.

SERVES 8

1 TABLESPOON CUMIN

1 TABLESPOON SMOKED PAPRIKA

1 TABLESPOON GARLIC

1 TABLESPOON ONION POWDER

1 TABLESPOON CHILI POWDER

2 TABLESPOONS COCONUT SUGAR

1 TEASPOON COARSE SALT

1/2 TEASPOON CAYENNE PEPPER

1   Mix all ingredients together and use for pork and chicken.

CITRUS VINAIGRETTE

This refreshing salad dressing can double as a marinade for chicken!

◇◇◇

SERVES 6

1 TEASPOON ORANGE ZEST

3 TABLESPOONS FRESH ORANGE JUICE

2 TEASPOONS DIJON MUSTARD

1 TABLESPOON HONEY

3 TABLESPOONS WHITE BALSAMIC VINEGAR

1/3 CUP OLIVE OIL

1   Whisk all the ingredients together and store in the refrigerator for up to one week.

CREOLE SEASONING

Think outside of the box with this seasoning blend. Of course it is perfect on all kinds of meats, but you have to try it on sweet potatoes and even asparagus!

SERVES 8

1/3 CUP SMOKED PAPRIKA

3 TABLESPOONS DRIED OREGANO

1 TABLESPOON COARSE GROUND BLACK PEPPER

2 TABLESPOONS DRIED BASIL

1 TEASPOON COARSE SALT

1/2 TEASPOON CAYENNE PEPPER

4 TEASPOONS ONION POWDER

4 TEASPOONS DRIED THYME

4 TEASPOONS GARLIC POWDER

1   Mix together and store in an airtight container.

HORSERADISH SAUCE

My mother always had horseradish sauce whenever we cooked a filet or prime rib. The addition of fresh herbs really takes this one over the top! Pssst! Try whipping it into some mashed cauliflower (see page 81)!

(see page 81)

SERVES 8

1/4 CUP ALMOND-BASED CREAM CHEESE

1/4 CUP ALMOND MILK

1/2 CUP OLIVE OIL MAYONNAISE

6 TABLESPOONS PREPARED HORSERADISH

1 TABLESPOON LEMON JUICE

3 TABLESPOONS CHOPPED FRESH PARSLEY

1/2 TEASPOON SALT

1/2 TEASPOON PEPPER

1   Stir all ingredients in mixing bowl until thoroughly combined.

2   Store in the refrigerator.

KETCHUP

Asking me to give up ketchup would be like asking me to give up water! But most are full of refined sugars, so I made my own! Thick and delicious and can stand up to any fries! Add a dash of cayenne for a kick!

SERVES 8

6 OUNCES TOMATO PASTE

1/2 CUP COCONUT SUGAR

2/3 CUP APPLE CIDER VINEGAR

1/2 TEASPOON FINE SEA SALT

1/2 TEASPOON ONION POWDER

1/2 TEASPOON GARLIC POWDER

1 CUPS WARM WATER

1   Combine all ingredients in a saucepan.

2   Simmer the sauce over low heat for 10 minutes. Stir well and chill.

MANGO CHUTNEY

I love mangos almost as much as I love peaches. This chutney is delicious on pork or chicken and is the perfect addition lamb!

SERVES 8

3 CUPS DICED MANGO

1/2 CUP COCONUT SUGAR

1/2 CUP DISTILLED VINEGAR

1/3 CUP DICED RED BELL PEPPER

1 TEASPOON MINCED GARLIC

2 TABLESPOONS FRESH GRATED GINGER

1/3 CUP CHOPPED VIDALIA ONION (OR ANY SWEET ONION)

1   Combine all ingredients in a saucepan and cook over medium heat for 5 minutes.

2   Reduce the heat and simmer for 10 more minutes. Be sure to stir the chutney every few minutes.

3   Remove from the heat and pour chutney into a blender. Pulse the mixture 5 times and serve. This can be served hot or cold.

4   Store the chutney in the refrigerator.

MAPLE AND BLUE CHEESE VINAIGRETTE

This salad dressing is over-the-top delicious. Try it on a grilled steak salad with some fresh figs!

SERVES 8

3 TABLESPOONS SHERRY VINEGAR

3 TABLESPOONS RED WINE VINEGAR

1/2 CUP OLIVE OIL

3 TABLESPOONS MAPLE SYRUP

3 TABLESPOONS CRUMBLED BLUE CHEESE

1   Whisk the vinegars, oil, and maple syrup together.

2   Stir in the blue cheese and serve.

ITALIAN SEASONING

Looking for the perfect go-to seasoning blend for vegetables? This is it! Mix it with a little olive oil and toss it with spaghetti squash or zucchini noodles.

SERVES 8

1 TABLESPOON GARLIC POWDER

1 TABLESPOON DRIED PARSLEY

1 TABLESPOON DRIED BASIL

1 TABLESPOON DRIED ROSEMARY

1 1/2 TEASPOONS DRIED OREGANO

1 TEASPOON CRUSHED RED PEPPER FLAKES

1/2 TEASPOON COARSE SALT

1   Mix all ingredients together and store in an airtight container. Perfect for beef, lamb, chicken, and vegetables.

2   When 1 teaspoon of this seasoning is mixed with 1/2 cup of olive oil, it can be used for dipping and marinating.

SWEET SOUTHERN BARBECUE SAUCE

Every part of the South has their signature sauce: spicy, sweet, tomato-based, mustard-based, and the list goes on. This one is a refined sugar-free twist on the one that I grew up with!

SERVES 6

1 CAN (12 OUNCES) TOMATO PASTE

1 3/4 CUPS WATER

1/4 CUP MOLASSES

1/2 CUP HONEY

1 1/2 TEASPOONS GARLIC POWDER

1 1/2 TEASPOONS ONION POWDER

1/4 CUP APPLE CIDER VINEGAR

1 TEASPOON CINNAMON

1 TEASPOON DRY MUSTARD

1/4 CUP COCONUT SUGAR

1   Combine the tomato paste and water into a large sauce pot over low heat. Stir frequently until the tomato paste and water are well combined.

2   Add the remaining ingredients and stir well until all ingredients are blended.

3   Simmer over low heat for 5 minutes.

4   Remove the sauce from the heat and serve immediately or store in the refrigerator.

SWEET TEA MARINADE

Southerners love our sweet tea, and this marinade packs tons of flavor that is perfect for pork or chicken. I like to reserve a little to use for basting when I grill.

SERVES 8

2 CUPS OF EARL GREY TEA, BREWED AND COOLED

2 TABLESPOONS HONEY

2 TABLESPOONS GRATED GINGER

1 TABLESPOON FRESH LIME JUICE

1 TABLESPOON LIME ZEST

1 TEASPOON GARLIC, MINCED

3 TABLESPOONS OLIVE OIL

1   Combine all ingredients together.

2   Marinate chicken or pork for 6-8 hours for maximum flavor.

TACO SEASONING

Fold a teaspoon of this seasoning blend into your guacamole, season beef or chicken for taco salads, or add some to a bowl of tomato soup. The possibilities are endless!

SERVES 8

1 TABLESPOON CHILI POWDER

1/2 TEASPOON GARLIC POWDER

1/4 TEASPOON ONION POWDER

1/2 TEASPOON OREGANO

1/4 TEASPOON CHIPOTLE POWDER

1/2 TEASPOON SMOKED PAPRIKA

1 1/2 TEASPOONS CUMIN

1 TEASPOON COARSE SALT

1   Combine all ingredients and store in an airtight container.

CHAPTER 3

—

SOUPS

CAULIFLOWER SOUP

This is creamy "potato" soup without the guilt. Perfect for a cold winter day!

SERVES 4

1 LARGE HEAD OF CAULIFLOWER

2 TABLESPOONS PECAN OR OLIVE OIL

1 CUP DICED VIDALIA ONION (OR ANY SWEET ONION)

3 CUPS ORGANIC CHICKEN BROTH

1 TABLESPOON GARLIC, MINCED

1 TEASPOON COARSE SALT

1 TEASPOON WHITE PEPPER

1 CUP COCONUT MILK

GREEN ONIONS, FOR GARNISH (OPTIONAL)

1   Wash the cauliflower and break the flower away from the stalk. Cut the cauliflower into 2-inch chunks and set aside.

2   In a large pot, heat the oil over medium heat. Add the onion and sauté for 3 minutes. Pour the chicken broth in with the onion.

3   Add the garlic, salt, pepper, and cauliflower to the pot and cook over medium heat for 15–20 minutes until the cauliflower is soft.

4   Puree the soup in a blender or with an emulsion blender.

5   Return the soup to the stove and add the coconut milk. Simmer for 15 minutes, garnish with green onions (if desired), and serve.

CHICKEN TACO SOUP

with Pico de Gallo

This soup is perfect as it is, but when you top it with fresh Pico de Gallo, it screams, "Oh my!"

SERVES 6

2 TABLESPOONS OLIVE OIL

2 1/2 POUNDS BONELESS, SKINLESS CHICKEN BREAST

4 CUPS ORGANIC CHICKEN BROTH

1 CUP DICED SWEET ONION

1 CAN (28 OUNCES) FIRE ROASTED TOMATOES

2 TABLESPOONS TACO SEASONING (SEE PAGE 37)

1 CAN (14.5 OUNCES) CHOPPED GREEN CHILES (OPTIONAL)

1   Heat the oil in a large skillet over medium heat. Cook the chicken in the skillet for about 5 minutes on each side.

2   Remove the chicken from the heat and place it in a heated slow cooker. Add all the remaining ingredients and cook on high for 4–6 hours.

3   Shred the chicken inside the slow cooker and stir well.

4   Serve with Pico de Gallo (see page 82).

CHILI

You can't cozy up by the fire with a bowl of soup any better than with this beanless chili. Sweet potatoes take center stage and will having you going back for more.

2 TABLESPOONS PECAN OIL

4 POUNDS SIRLOIN BEEF, CUT INTO BITE-SIZE PIECES

2 CANS (28 OUNCES) CRUSHED TOMATOES

1 1/2 CUPS CHOPPED GREEN BELL PEPPER

2 CUPS CHOPPED SWEET ONION

1/2 CUP PACKED COCONUT SUGAR

1 TABLESPOON GROUND CUMIN

3 TABLESPOONS CHILI POWDER

1 TABLESPOON DRIED BASIL

1 TABLESPOON LEMON ZEST

2 CUPS SWEET POTATO, PEELED AND CUBED

1 Pour oil in a large pot and brown the beef.

2 Add the remaining ingredients, except for the sweet potatoes, and simmer for 2 hours, stirring every 30 minutes.

3 Add the sweet potatoes and cook for another hour. Serve hot.

SHRIMP AND GRITS

Never has there been a dish more Southern! Just like the South, the recipe varies from one part of the South to the others. Mine takes a Georgia twist with the incorporation of vidalia onion, local olive oil, and local grits.

SERVES 4

4 CUPS CHICKEN BROTH

1/2 TEASPOON PEPPER

1 CUP COARSE GROUND GRITS

8 OUNCES PARMESAN CHEESE, GRATED

2 TABLESPOONS OLIVE OIL

1 LARGE VIDALIA ONION (OR ANY SWEET ONION), CHOPPED

1/2 TEASPOON COARSE SALT

1 POUND LARGE SHRIMP, PEELED AND DEVEINED

1/4 CUP OLIVE OIL

2 CLOVES OF GARLIC, MINCED

2 TABLESPOONS CHOPPED FRESH ROSEMARY

1   For the grits, bring the chicken broth and pepper to a boil.

2   Add the grits to the broth and cook covered over low-medium heat for 1 hour, stirring frequently. Add water 1/4 cup at a time as needed during the cooking to keep the grits from sticking.

3   During the last 15 minutes of cooking, add the parmesan cheese and stir to allow it to dissolve into the grits.

4   For the onions, pour the olive oil in a skillet over low-medium heat and add the onion and salt. Cook for 15 minutes until caramelized.

5   Preheat the oven to 400 degrees. Spread the shrimp on a greased baking sheet.

6   Mix the olive oil, garlic, and rosemary and pour over the shrimp. Roast the shrimp for 8 to 10 minutes.

7   Ladle the grits into large bowls and divide the onions and shrimp evenly among the grits.

STRAWBERRY SOUP

This soup is the perfect for a summer luncheon, shower, or party. Sweet strawberries and a hint of fresh mint.

SERVES 6

2 POUNDS FRESH STRAWBERRIES, WASHED
  AND HULLED

16 OUNCES COCONUT MILK

5 OUNCES VANILLA GREEK YOGURT

1/2 TEASPOON PURE VANILLA EXTRACT

FRESH MINT FOR GARNISH (OPTIONAL)

1   Combine all the ingredients in a blender until smooth.

2   Serve in chilled bowls and garnish with fresh mint.

BUTTERNUT SQUASH AND SWEET POTATO SOUP

Warm and comforting with a hint of curry. This is a favorite all fall and winter long, especially at your Thanksgiving table.

SERVES 6

3 TABLESPOONS UNSALTED ALL-NATURAL BUTTER OR GHEE

1 CLOVE OF GARLIC, MINCED

2 LARGE VIDALIA ONIONS (OR ANY SWEET ONIONS), CHOPPED

3 MEDIUM SWEET POTATOES, CUBED

1 MEDIUM BUTTERNUT SQUASH PEELED, SEEDED AND CUBED

32 OUNCES ORGANIC CHICKEN BROTH

1 1/2 TEASPOONS CURRY POWDER

1 TEASPOON GRATED NUTMEG

1 1/2 TEASPOONS COARSE SALT

1 CUP ALMOND MILK

1   Melt the butter in a large stock pot over medium heat. Add the garlic, onion, sweet potatoes, and squash. Cook for 10 minutes.

2   Pour the chicken broth over the vegetables and add curry, nutmeg, and salt. Stir well and cook for 45 minutes.

3   With an immersion blender, puree the soup until it is smooth.

4   Pour in the almond milk and stir to blend. If desired, top with a dollop of greek yogurt and crispy prosciutto to serve.

SEAFOOD GUMBO

You can't have gumbo without a roux. My gluten-free roux gives this gumbo depth and richness. I like mine packed with crab and shrimp, but you can add your favorites for your own twist.

SERVES 6

GUMBO

1 TABLESPOON BUTTER	6 CUPS SEAFOOD STOCK
1 LARGE SWEET ONION, CHOPPED	1/2 TEASPOON CAYENNE PEPPER
1 BELL PEPPER, CHOPPED	1/4 TEASPOON DRIED ROSEMARY
1 CUP CELERY, CHOPPED	1/4 TEASPOON DRIED THYME
1 CLOVE OF GARLIC, CHOPPED	1 BAY LEAF
6 OUNCES TOMATO PASTE	1 POUND LARGE SHRIMP, PEELED AND DEVEINED
14 OUNCES DICED TOMATOES	
8 OUNCES TOMATO SAUCE	12 OUNCES LUMP CRABMEAT, FLAKED

1   In a large skillet, melt the butter over medium heat. Add the onion, bell pepper, celery, and garlic to the skillet, cooking until tender.

2   Remove the skillet from the heat and set it aside while you make the roux.

ROUX

1 STICK BUTTER	1/2 CUP ALMOND FLOUR
1/2 CUP OLIVE OIL	

1   Melt the butter in a large stock pot over medium heat. Add the oil to the butter and whisk the almond flour into the butter and oil.

2   Whisk constantly for 10 to 15 minutes until the roux becomes a dark blond color.

3   Add the cooked vegetables to the roux and then begin adding the tomato paste, diced tomatoes, tomato sauce, and seafood stock.

4   With the heat still on medium, add the remaining herbs and cayenne pepper. Cover the pot and allow the gumbo to simmer for 45 minutes.

5   Add the shrimp and crabmeat, and cook for 15 more minutes. Serve hot.

OYSTER STEW

This was my Grandmother Mimi's recipe and a Christmas Eve favorite in our family. Simple comfort food.

SERVES 4

1/2 CUP VERY FINELY CHOPPED SWEET ONION

4 TABLESPOONS OLIVE OIL

1 PINT FRESH OYSTERS (WITH JUICE)

1 TEASPOON SALT

1/2 TEASPOON BLACK PEPPER

1 QUART OF COCONUT MILK

1 CUP COOKED, DICED RED POTATOES

1   Sauté the onions in the olive oil over medium heat.

2   Add the oysters with the juice, salt, and pepper to the oil. Cook on low until the oysters' edges begin to curl.

3   Add the coconut milk and potato to the oysters and heat thoroughly but do not boil.

4   Remove from the heat and serve hot.

CHAPTER 4

—

SALADS

CAJUN POTATO SALAD

You can't have a cookout or barbecue without an amazing potato salad. Mine combines spicy andouille sausage and sweet potatoes with a tangy vinaigrette. No heavy mayonnaise in this recipe!

SERVES 8

2 POUNDS SWEET POTATOES, CUT INTO 1-INCH CUBES

6 TABLESPOONS APPLE CIDER VINEGAR

4 TABLESPOONS OLIVE OIL

1 TABLESPOON CREOLE MUSTARD

2 CLOVES OF GARLIC, MINCED

1/2 TEASPOON SALT

1/2 TEASPOON CAYENNE PEPPER

3/4 POUND CAJUN TURKEY SAUSAGE, SLICED

1/2 CUP CHOPPED VIDALIA ONION (OR ANY SWEET ONION)

1/2 CUP CHOPPED SCALLIONS

1/4 CUP CHOPPED PARSLEY

1   Preheat the oven to 400 degrees.

2   On a baking sheet lined with foil and sprayed with cooking spray, roast the sweet potatoes until tender, about 35 minutes.

3   Whisk the apple cider vinegar, olive oil, mustard, garlic, salt, and cayenne pepper together and set aside.

4   In a skillet over medium heat, brown the sausage and onion together until the onions are tender. Add the sweet potatoes to the sausage mixture.

5   Pour the liquid mixture into the skillet and stir into the potatoes and sausage. Remove the skillet from the heat.

6   Add the scallions and parsley, toss well, and serve.

CUCUMBER SALAD

Light and refreshing. This salad is perfect for all of those summer cucumbers. What's even better? After a few days, they become pickles!

SERVES 8

4 LARGE CUCUMBERS

1 CUP APPLE CIDER VINEGAR

2 TABLESPOONS OLIVE OIL

1/2 CUP HONEY

1/2 TEASPOON SALT

1/2 TEASPOON DRY MUSTARD

1/2 TEASPOON CELERY SEEDS

1   Slice the cucumbers into coins and place in a large bowl.

2   In a small bowl, whisk remaining ingredients together and pour over the cucumbers.

3   Cover, chill, and allow to marinate for 2–3 hours before serving.

CURRIED GRILLED QUAIL SALAD

Don't let chicken salad always take center stage. I love to use sweet and delicate quail for my recipe. The curry, pineapple, and macadamia nuts give it a real tropical flavor!

SERVES 4

6 BONELESS, SKINLESS QUAIL BREASTS

2 TABLESPOONS OLIVE OIL

1/2 TEASPOON COARSE SALT

1/2 CUP OLIVE OIL MAYONNAISE

1/2 CUP MANGO CHUTNEY (SEE PAGE 30)

2 TEASPOONS MINCED GARLIC

2 TABLESPOONS CURRY POWDER

1 CAN (8 OUNCES) PINEAPPLE TIDBITS IN NATURAL JUICE

3/4 CUP CHOPPED MACADAMIA NUTS

1   Brush the quail with olive oil and season with salt.

2   Grill the quail over medium-high heat for 3 minutes on each side. Allow to rest for 5 minutes before cutting into strips.

3   Combine the mayonnaise, Mango Chutney, garlic, curry powder, pineapple, and nuts together in a large bowl.

4   Toss the quail in the mixture and chill for 2–3 hours before serving.

MARINATED MUSHROOM SALAD

No lettuce required for this amazing salad! This flavorful dish is perfect for serving year round and holds up great in hot weather.

SERVES 6

SALAD

2 1/2 QUARTS WATER

3 POUNDS SMALL FRESH WHITE MUSHROOMS

JUICE OF 2 LEMONS

1 CUP CHOPPED GREEN BELL PEPPER

1 CUP DICED SWEET ONION

1/2 CUP SLICED KALAMATA OLIVES

2 TABLESPOONS CHOPPED FRESH BASIL

DRESSING

1/2 CUP OLIVE OIL

1/2 CUP WHITE BALSAMIC VINEGAR

1 CLOVE OF GARLIC, MINCED

1/2 TEASPOON SALT

1   In a large pot, bring the water to a boil. Add the mushrooms and lemon juice to the boiling water. Cook for 3 minutes.

2   Drain the mushrooms and allow them to cool.

3   In a large bowl, add the remaining salad ingredients except the basil and stir them together.

4   Whisk the dressing ingredients together and pour over the salad. Sprinkle the basil over the salad, toss well, and serve.

ONION AND MUSHROOM SALAD

with Pecan Truffle Vinaigrette

I love a salad that can really stand on its own. Meaty mushrooms, sweet onion, and a pecan truffle vinaigrette really make this one stand out. Did you know that pecan truffles are found at the base of pecan trees and used to make delicious pecan truffle oil?

SERVES 4

VINAIGRETTE

3 TABLESPOONS BALSAMIC VINEGAR

4 TABLESPOONS PECAN OIL

1 TABLESPOON PECAN TRUFFLE OIL

1   Mix together and set aside.

SALAD

6 OUNCES PORTABELLA MUSHROOMS

2 TABLESPOONS PECAN OIL

2 TABLESPOONS PECAN TRUFFLE OIL

1 VIDALIA ONION (OR ANY SWEET ONION), THINLY SLICED

4 CUPS ARUGULA

1/4 CUP SHREDDED PECORINO CHEESE

1   Sauté the mushrooms in the pecan oil over medium heat. Remove the mushrooms from the skillet and set them aside.

2   Add the truffle oil to the skillet and caramelize the onions.

3   Place the arugula on a large platter and arrange the mushrooms and onions over the arugula.

4   Sprinkle the cheese on top, drizzle with the vinaigrette, and serve.

QUINOA SALAD

My absolute favorite salad to make up for a busy week! It makes the perfect side dish or you can top it with the meat or fish of your choice, and it transforms into the perfect main dish.

❮❮

SERVES 6

1 CUP QUINOA, COOKED AND COOLED

1 MEDIUM CUCUMBER, SEEDED AND CHOPPED

1 CUP CHOPPED GRAPE TOMATOES

1 RED BELL PEPPER, CHOPPED

1 GREEN BELL PEPPER, CHOPPED

1 RED ONION, DICED FINELY

1 CUP HALVED KALAMATA OLIVES

6 OUNCES FETA CHEESE

1/4 CUP OLIVE OIL

1/4 CUP WHITE BALSAMIC VINEGAR

1/2 TEASPOON DRIED OREGANO

1 TEASPOON HONEY

1/2 TEASPOON COARSE SALT

1/2 TEASPOON BLACK PEPPER

8 OUNCES OF SALMON, GRILLED CHICKEN, OR SHRIMP (OPTIONAL)

1   Toss the quinoa, cucumber, tomatoes, peppers, onion, olives, and feta in a large bowl.

2   In a small bowl, mix the olive oil, vinegar, oregano, honey, salt, and pepper together to make the dressing and pour over the salad.

3   Top with your choice of meat or eat plain.

WALDORF FRUIT SALAD

This is the perfect salad for the holidays. You can make it in advance, and it will keep in the refrigerator for several days.

SERVES 8

1 CUP DRIED CRANBERRIES

2/3 CUP HALVED GREEN GRAPES

2/3 CUP HALVED RED GRAPES

1 CUP CHOPPED APPLE

1/3 CUP GOLDEN RAISINS

1 CUP CHOPPED CELERY

1/2 CUP CHOPPED PECANS OR WALNUTS

1/2 CUP ALMOND-BASED VANILLA YOGURT

1/2 CUP ALMOND-BASED CREAM CHEESE

1/2 CUP MAPLE SYRUP

2 TABLESPOONS ORANGE ZEST

1 Place the fruit, celery, and nuts in a large bowl.

2 In another bowl, stir together the yogurt, cream cheese, maple syrup, and orange zest then pour it over the fruit mixture.

3 Stir well and serve!

CHAPTER 5

—

SIDES

BRUSSELS SPROUTS

with Mustard Glaze

The mustard sauce gives these little beauties a zing that will have your kids asking for more!

5 CUPS WATER

1 TABLESPOON COARSE SALT

4 CUPS BRUSSELS SPROUTS, WASHED, STEMS TRIMMED

2 TABLESPOONS UNSALTED BUTTER

1 TABLESPOON COARSE GROUND GRAIN MUSTARD

1 TABLESPOON HONEY

1/2 TEASPOON FRESH GROUND BLACK PEPPER

1   Bring salted water to a boil and place the brussels sprouts into the water.

2   Boil the sprouts for 8 minutes. Drain the sprouts well.

3   Melt the butter in a large skillet and stir in the mustard, honey, and pepper.

4   Add the sprouts and toss well to coat.

CRANBERRY SALSA

Move over plain cranberry sauce—this salsa is taking center stage at the Thanksgiving table. Try some on leftover turkey sandwiches!

SERVES 8

2 CUPS WATER

12 OUNCES FRESH CRANBERRIES

1 CUP COCONUT SUGAR

1/4 CUP CHOPPED CILANTRO

1-2 TABLESPOONS FINELY CHOPPED JALAPEÑO

1/4 CUP CHOPPED ONION

2 TABLESPOONS ORANGE ZEST

1/2 TEASPOON COARSE SALT

1   Bring the water to a boil in a large saucepan and add the cranberries. Cook the cranberries until they open.

2   Drain the cranberries and allow them to cool completely.

3   Toss the cooled cranberries with the remaining ingredients and serve.

SAUTÉED KALE

My father always planted a garden when I was growing up. Kale is one of the most versatile greens, and it packs a nutritional punch as well.

2 TABLESPOONS OLIVE OIL

1 CLOVE OF GARLIC, MINCED

1/4 CUP WATER

1 POUND KALE

1 TEASPOON SALT

PINCH OF RED PEPPER FLAKES

1   Heat the olive oil in a large saucepan over medium-high heat. Add the garlic and cook 3–4 minutes.

2   Raise the heat to high, add the water and kale, and toss to combine. Cover and cook for 5 minutes.

3   Remove the cover and continue to cook. Stir until all the water has evaporated.

4   Remove the kale from the heat, sprinkle with salt and red pepper flakes, and serve.

"FRIED" GREEN TOMATOES

Yes, you can still have those summer green beauties without deep frying or gluten. I promise, you will never know the difference!

◇◇◇

SERVES 4

2 MEDIUM GREEN TOMATOES

1 CUP ALMOND MILK

1 CUP ALMOND FLOUR

1 TEASPOON COARSE SALT

1 TEASPOON COARSE GROUND BLACK PEPPER

1 TEASPOON GARLIC POWDER

2 TABLESPOONS PECAN OIL

1   Preheat the oven to 425 degrees.

2   Cut the ends and tops off the tomatoes. Slice the tomatoes to 1/4 inch in thickness, making about 4 slices per tomato.

3   Pour the almond milk in a shallow bowl. Pour the flour and seasonings into a large Ziploc bag or brown paper bag.

4   Pour the oil in a large cast iron skillet and spread it evenly to cover the bottom of the skillet.

5   Dip the tomato slices one at a time into the almond milk and shake off the excess milk.

6   Quickly toss the tomato into the flour mixture and coat on both sides, then shake off the excess flour. Do this with all the slices and arrange them in the skillet.

7   Place the skillet in the oven and bake for 15 minutes.

8   Flip the tomato slices over and bake them for another 15-20 minutes to get really crispy tomatoes.

GREEN BEAN CASSEROLE

A Thanksgiving classic side dish with a healthy remake!

◇◇

SERVES 8

1 TABLESPOON OLIVE OIL

1 LARGE ONION, SLICED

2 TABLESPOONS BUTTER

2 CLOVES OF GARLIC, MINCED

1 TABLESPOON ALMOND FLOUR

1 CUP VEGETABLE BROTH

32 OUNCES GREEN BEANS, FROZEN

16 OUNCES FRESH MUSHROOMS

4 TABLESPOONS GRATED PARMESAN CHEESE

1   Preheat the oven to 350 degrees.

2   Heat the olive oil in a large skillet over medium heat. Sauté the onion until tender, remove it from the skillet, and set aside.

3   Melt the butter in the same skillet and add the garlic. Cook the garlic for 1 minute.

4   Sprinkle the flour into the butter mixture and whisk in the vegetable broth. Cook, stirring constantly, for 3 minutes.

5   Pour the green beans and mushrooms into a 9x13 baking dish and pour the mixture evenly over the top.

6   Arrange the onions evenly on the top and bake for 30 minutes.

7   Sprinkle the parmesan cheese on top and bake for 5 more minutes. Serve hot.

MAPLE-GLAZED CARROTS

These are so sweet and delicious, you can eat them like candy!

SERVES 6

3 POUNDS BABY CUT CARROTS OR TRI-COLOR CARROTS

4 TABLESPOONS BUTTER, MELTED

1/4 CUP MAPLE SYRUP

2 TEASPOONS NUTMEG

2 TEASPOONS COARSE SALT

1   Preheat the oven to 350 degrees.

2   Arrange the carrots in a greased 9x13 baking dish.

3   Mix the butter, maple syrup, and nutmeg together and pour over the carrots.

4   Sprinkle with the coarse salt and bake for 1 hour, stirring halfway through.

MASHED CAULIFLOWER

No one loves mashed potatoes more than my oldest son, Christopher. When he gave these the stamp of approval over mashed potatoes, I knew I had a winner!

SERVES 6

1 LARGE HEAD OF CAULIFLOWER

1/4 CUP GHEE

1 TABLESPOON CHOPPED FRESH ROSEMARY

1 TABLESPOON MINCED GARLIC

1/2 CUP ALMOND-BASED CREAM CHEESE

1/2 CUP CHICKEN BROTH

1 TEASPOON COARSE SALT

1 TEASPOON COARSE GROUND BLACK PEPPER

1   Break the cauliflower into large pieces and place in a pot of boiling water. Cook the cauliflower until it is tender.

2   Drain the cauliflower and place it in a large bowl.

3   Add the remaining ingredients and, using a hand mixer, whip everything together and serve.

PICO DE GALLO

Talk about the all-around nutrition-popping topping! Full of veggies and heart-healthy avocado, you can't go wrong. Add to soup, meats, poultry, or salad, or serve as an appetizer.

SERVES 8

2 CUPS DICED FRESH TOMATOES

1/2 CUP DICED VIDALIA (OR ANY SWEET ONION)

2 TABLESPOONS FRESH LIME JUICE

1/2 CUP CHOPPED CILANTRO

1/2 TEASPOON COARSE SALT

1 AVOCADO, CUBED

1   Mix all ingredients well and serve.

ROSEMARY ROASTED SWEET POTATO FRIES

If I had only one herb that I could use it would have to be rosemary. Simply delicious and a family favorite.

SERVES 8

4 LARGE SWEET POTATOES

1/4 CUP OLIVE OIL

4 TABLESPOONS CHOPPED FRESH ROSEMARY

1 TABLESPOON COARSE SALT

1   Preheat the oven to 400 degrees.

2   Wash sweet potatoes and cut them each into approximately 8 large wedges horizontally.

3   Toss the potatoes, olive oil, rosemary, and salt together, coating the potatoes well.

4   Arrange the sweet potatoes on a baking sheet. Bake for 35 minutes or until crispy.

SPAGHETTI SQUASH

with Pecan Truffle Oil and Herbs

I can't grow a flower to save my life, but herbs I grow in abundance. This dish is one of my favorite ways to use them.

◇◇

SERVES 4

1 MEDIUM SPAGHETTI SQUASH	2 TABLESPOONS CHOPPED PARSLEY
1 TABLESPOON PECAN OIL	2 TABLESPOONS CHOPPED FRESH OREGANO
1 TEASPOON COARSE SALT	2 TABLESPOONS PECAN TRUFFLE OIL
1 TEASPOON COARSE GROUND BLACK PEPPER	1/2 CUP GRATED PARMESAN CHEESE (OPTIONAL)

1   Preheat the oven to 350 degrees.

2   Cut the squash in half and remove the seeds.

3   Place the squash on a baking sheet. Rub the pecan oil evenly on both halves of the squash and sprinkle evenly with salt and pepper.

4   Roast the squash in the oven for 45 minutes. Remove the squash from the oven and scrape the flesh into a large bowl with a fork.

5   Add the parsley, oregano, pecan truffle oil, and parmesan to the bowl, toss well, and serve.

SUMMER VEGETABLE RATATOUILLE

When summer vegetables and fresh herbs come together, it's an irresistible combination. A little visit to the farmers' market makes for a perfect side dish!

SERVES 8

1 EGGPLANT, PEELED AND CUBED

2 LARGE SUMMER TOMATOES, SEEDED AND CHOPPED

2 YELLOW SUMMER SQUASHES, CUBED

1 LARGE VIDALIA ONION (OR ANY SWEET ONION), CHOPPED

2 ZUCCHINI SQUASHES, CUBED

2 TABLESPOONS CHOPPED FRESH OREGANO

2 TABLESPOONS CHOPPED FRESH PARSLEY

1/4 CUP OLIVE OIL

1 TEASPOON COARSE SALT

1 TEASPOON COARSE GROUND BLACK PEPPER

1   Preheat the oven to 400 degrees.

2   Combine all ingredients in a large bowl and stir well to coat all the vegetables with the oil, salt, and pepper.

3   Pour the mixture into a greased cast iron skillet and roast the vegetables in the oven for 35–40 minutes.

TWICE-BAKED SWEET POTATOES

No one can resist the sweet deliciousness of maple syrup and pecans in these potatoes. Make up a few and freeze them for busy weekday meals or for your holiday dinners!

SERVES 8

4 SWEET POTATOES, WASHED AND DRIED

OLIVE OIL

4 TABLESPOONS GHEE (OR BUTTER)

1/3 CUP COCONUT MILK

2 TABLESPOONS MAPLE SYRUP

1/3 CUP TOASTED PECANS

1 TEASPOON GROUND CINNAMON

1/2 TEASPOON GROUND NUTMEG

1 Preheat the oven to 400 degrees.

2 Rub sweet potatoes with olive oil. Place potatoes on a baking sheet and roast for 1 hour. Allow to cool slightly so that you can handle them safely.

3 Cut off the top 1/4 of each potato and scoop out the flesh. Be sure to leave enough of the potato inside so that the skin does not tear.

4 Lower the oven temperature to 350 degrees. Mix the potato flesh, ghee, coconut milk, maple syrup, pecans, cinnamon, and nutmeg together.

5 Stuff the mixture evenly back into the skins.

6 Return the potatoes to the oven for about 20 minutes to warm thoroughly before serving.

CHAPTER 6

MAIN
DISHES

CRAB CAKES

with Remoulade Sauce

I never met a crab cake that I didn't like, and this one is a real a winner. Classic remoulade sauce on the side, and you will feel like you are in The Big Easy!

SERVES 4

CRAB CAKES

1 POUND LUMP CRABMEAT, PICKED OVER AND
   SHELLS REMOVED

1 1/2 CUPS QUINOA, COOKED AND COOLED

1/4 CUP FINELY CHOPPED GREEN BELL
   PEPPER

1/4 CUP FINELY DICED SWEET ONION

JUICE OF 1 LEMON

1 TABLESPOON CREOLE MUSTARD

2 TABLESPOONS OLIVE OIL MAYONNAISE

1 EGG, BEATEN

1   Mix all ingredients in a large bowl.

2   Shape into 12 cakes and place on a greased baking sheet. Place the crab cakes in the refrigerator for 2
    hours.

3   Preheat the oven to 400 degrees. Place the crab cakes in the oven for 15 minutes.

4   Serve with Remoulade Sauce.

REMOULADE SAUCE

1/2 CUP OLIVE OIL MAYONNAISE

1/2 CUP ALMOND-BASED CREAM CHEESE

1 TABLESPOON MINCED GARLIC

1/2 CUP CHOPPED SCALLIONS

2 TABLESPOONS CREOLE MUSTARD

1 TABLESPOON LEMON ZEST

1 TEASPOON LEMON JUICE

1   Combine all ingredients together and serve.

CREOLE OVEN-FRIED CHICKEN

Spicy creole seasoning and a cast-iron skillet are the secrets to this delicious chicken!

SERVES 6

3 POUNDS BONELESS, SKINLESS CHICKEN BREASTS

2 TABLESPOONS CREOLE SEASONING (SEE PAGE 25)

1/3 CUP PECAN OIL

1/3 CUP ALMOND FLOUR

1   Preheat the oven to 425 degrees.

2   Season the chicken with the Creole Seasoning.

3   Pour the oil into a large cast iron skillet and set it in the oven for 4 minutes.

4   Pour the almond flour into a large plastic bag. Place the chicken in the bag and shake the bag to coat the chicken.

5   Carefully remove the skillet from the oven, place the chicken in the hot skillet, and return it to the oven.

6   Cook the chicken for 15 minutes, and then turn the chicken over to cook the other side. Cook for 25 more minutes.

FILET OF BEEF

with Italian Salsa Verde

I love the idea of a sauce for steak that is fresh and crisp. This herb-packed sauce really is a perfect addition to enhance, not cover up, the flavor of the beef.

SERVES 6

FILET OF BEEF

3 POUNDS FILET OF BEEF TENDERLOIN

2 TABLESPOONS OLIVE OIL

2 TEASPOONS KOSHER SALT

1 TEASPOON BLACK PEPPER

1   Remove the beef from the refrigerator and allow it to sit for 30 minutes.

2   Preheat the oven to 275 degrees.

3   Pat the beef dry with a paper towel. Place the beef on a baking sheet and rub the whole filet with the olive oil.

4   Sprinkle the beef with the salt and pepper. Roast the beef for 1 hour and 15 minutes.

5   Remove the beef from the oven and allow it to rest for 20 minutes before slicing.

6   Serve with the Italian Salsa Verde on the side.

ITALIAN SALSA VERDE

2 CUPS FLAT-LEAF PARSLEY

1/4 CUP FRESH OREGANO

JUICE OF 1 LEMON

3 TABLESPOONS OF CAPERS, DRAINED

2 CLOVES OF GARLIC

PINCH OF RED PEPPER FLAKES

1/2 CUP OLIVE OIL

1   Combine all ingredients in the blender until smooth.

GRILLED LAMB CHOPS

with Sweet Onion Sauce

Lamb doesn't have to be saved for a special occasion—although it will feel like a holiday when you serve this delicious dish!

SERVES 8

GRILLED LAMB CHOPS

4 TABLESPOONS OLIVE OIL

1 TEASPOON FRESH ROSEMARY, FINELY CHOPPED

JUICE OF 1 LEMON

8 LAMB CHOPS, CUT INTO 1/2-INCH THICK SLICES

1   Combine the olive oil, rosemary, and lemon juice together.

2   Place lamb chops in a shallow baking dish.

3   Rub both sides of the chops with the mixture. Cover the chops with plastic wrap and refrigerate for 1 hour.

4   Grill the chops over medium heat, turning every 5 minutes until they reach an internal temperature of 145 degrees.

5   Remove the chops from the grill and serve with Sweet Onion Sauce.

SWEET ONION SAUCE

1 LARGE VIDALIA ONION (OR ANY SWEET ONION), DICED

1/4 CUP OLIVE OIL

1/4 CUP COCONUT SUGAR

2 TABLESPOONS FRESH ROSEMARY, CHOPPED FINELY

1/4 CUP BALSAMIC VINEGAR

1   In a skillet, combine the onion, olive oil, coconut sugar, and rosemary.

2   Cook over medium-low heat to gently cook the onions until tender and just beginning to caramelize.

3   Remove the mixture from the heat and stir in the balsamic vinegar until well blended.

4   Serve the sauce warm for wonderful flavor.

HERBED PORK TENDERLOIN

This is my go-to Sunday supper dish. It appeals to every palate.

SERVES 8

1 TABLESPOON COARSE SALT

2 TEASPOONS COARSE GROUND BLACK PEPPER

4 CLOVES OF GARLIC, MINCED

2 TABLESPOONS OLIVE OIL

3 TEASPOONS CHOPPED FRESH THYME

3 TEASPOONS CHOPPED FRESH ROSEMARY

4 1-POUND PORK TENDERLOINS

2 EXTRA TABLESPOONS OLIVE OIL FOR THE SKILLET

1 Preheat the oven to 400 degrees.

2 Combine the salt, pepper, garlic, olive oil, thyme, and rosemary together. Rub the mixture entirely over each tenderloin.

3 Pour 2 tablespoons olive oil in a cast iron skillet. Sear each side of the tenderloins over medium-high heat until golden brown.

4 Place the pan into the oven and cook the tenderloins for about 20 minutes more until the internal temperature reaches 140 degrees in the thickest part of the tenderloin.

5 Remove the tenderloin from the oven, cover with foil, and allow it to rest for 20 minutes before slicing.

PECAN-CRUSTED CATFISH

My grandmother, Mimi, loved to have a fish fry better than anyone else I know. This is my non-fried version of fried catfish, but I think she would have approved!

SERVES 4

2 TABLESPOONS PECAN OIL

2 EGGS

1 TEASPOON COARSE SALT

1 TEASPOON COARSE GROUND BLACK PEPPER

1 CUP PECAN MEAL

4 6-OUNCE CATFISH FILETS

1   Preheat the oven for 400 degrees.

2   Spread the oil on a foil-lined baking sheet.

3   Whip the eggs in a shallow bowl.

4   Combine the salt, pepper, and pecan meal in another shallow bowl.

5   Dredge the catfish in the egg, allowing the excess to drip off. Dredge the catfish in the pecan meal mixture and lay it on the baking sheet.

6   Bake the catfish for 10 to 12 minutes. Serve hot.

ROASTED CORNISH HENS

with Georgia Peach Glaze

Sweet Georgia peaches are the secret to this dish. This is a perfect dish when you want to impress your guest without a lot of work!

SERVES 6

GEORGIA PEACH GLAZE

1/2 CUP HONEY

1/2 CUP PEELED AND CHOPPED FRESH
    PEACHES

1 TABLESPOON WHITE BALSAMIC VINEGAR

JUICE OF 1 ORANGE

1   Mix the ingredients together and put over low heat until the peaches are soft and all ingredients are mixed well.

2   Puree the mixture in the blender.

3   Divide the mixture in half. Use one half for basting the hens, and the other half can be served alongside them.

ROASTED CORNISH HENS

6 CORNISH HENS

1 TEASPOON SALT

1 TEASPOON PEPPER

1 NAVEL ORANGE

1 VIDALIA ONION (OR ANY SWEET ONION)

1/2 RECIPE GEORGIA PEACH GLAZE, FOR
    BASTING

1   Preheat the oven to 425 degrees.

2   Wash and pat the hens dry. Sprinkle the hens evenly with salt and pepper.

3   Cut the orange and the onion into 6 wedges and place one piece of each in the cavity of each hen.

4   Roast the hens in the oven for 35 to 40 minutes. When the hens have cooked for 15 minutes, begin basting them with the Georgia Peach Glaze every 10 minutes.

5   Remove the hens from the oven, baste them again, and allow to rest 10 minutes.

ARNOLD PALMER QUAIL

Next time you want a signature dish to serve during the Master's, try this twist!

SERVES 4

4 EARL GREY TEA BAGS   8 QUAIL BREASTS
12 OUNCES WATER   1 TEASPOON SALT
1/4 CUP HONEY   1 TEASPOON PEPPER
1/2 CUP LEMON JUICE

1   Brew the tea and stir in the honey. Let the tea cool completely.

2   Add the lemon juice to the tea and chill.

3   Arrange the quail in a 9x13 baking dish. Pour the chilled tea mixture over the quail and allow to marinate overnight in the refrigerator.

4   Remove the quail breasts from the marinade and pat them dry. Sprinkle the quail evenly with salt and pepper.

5   Grill the quail over medium-hot coals for about 8 minutes per side and serve.

SALMON

with Ginger Lime Sauce

Salmon is one of the easiest and quickest main dishes you can make. Just because it is easy doesn't mean it has to be plain. Serve it with my delicious Ginger Lime Sauce, but you better make extra! This sauce is so delicious that you will want it to serve alongside stir fry veggies, on chicken, with shellfish, and as a delicious salad dressing!

SERVES 4

GINGER LIME SAUCE

1/2 CUP OLIVE OIL MAYONNAISE

1/4 CUP HONEY

1/4 CUP FRESHLY SQUEEZED LIME JUICE

1 CLOVE OF GARLIC, MINCED

1 TABLESPOON GRATED FRESH GINGER

1/2 TEASPOON SALT

1   In a bowl combine the mayonnaise, honey, lime juice, garlic, ginger, and salt.

2   Mix well, cover, and chill for 30 minutes to allow the flavors to develop.

SALMON

2 POUNDS FRESH SALMON FILET, SKIN
   REMOVED

2 TABLESPOONS OLIVE OIL

1/2 TEASPOON SALT

1/2 TEASPOON PEPPER

1   Preheat the oven to 425 degrees.

2   Place the salmon on a baking sheet lined with foil. Drizzle the olive oil over the salmon and sprinkle with salt and pepper.

3   Bake in the oven for 20-25 minutes.

4   Serve the salmon with the Ginger Lime Sauce drizzled across the top.

SEAFOOD OMELET

Breakfast, brunch, lunch, or dinner this omelet is a hit. I love to have breakfast for dinner on a busy weeknight.

SERVES 6

5 EGGS

2 TABLESPOONS MILK

2 TABLESPOONS BUTTER

1/4 POUND COOKED SHRIMP, PEELED, DEVEINED, AND CHOPPED INTO LARGE BITS

1/4 CUP CHOPPED SCALLIONS

4 OUNCES LUMP CRABMEAT

4 OUNCES ALMOND-BASED CREAM CHEESE AT ROOM TEMPERATURE

2 TABLESPOONS PARMESAN CHEESE (OPTIONAL)

1 Preheat the oven to 350 degrees.

2 In a large bowl, whisk together the eggs and milk.

3 Melt the butter in an oven-proof skillet or omelet pan. Sauté the shrimp in the butter until pink.

4 Remove the skillet from the heat. Pour the egg mixture over the shrimp.

5 Add the scallions and crabmeat evenly across the top of the egg mixture. Crumble the cream cheese evenly across the egg mixture and sprinkle with the parmesan.

6 Place the skillet in the oven for 15–20 minutes, then serve immediately.

TRUFFLE AND ROSEMARY CHICKEN

Think of chicken as a delicious canvas, ready to take on whatever flavor you want to give it. It is the one meat that can handle any variation and pairs with everything. Rich and herbaceous, this one will be a favorite.

SERVES 2

2 BONELESS, SKINLESS CHICKEN BREASTS

1 TEASPOON COARSE SALT

1 TEASPOON COARSE GROUND BLACK PEPPER

2 TABLESPOONS PECAN OIL

1 TABLESPOON MINCED GARLIC

1/2 CUP CHICKEN BROTH

2 TABLESPOONS CHOPPED FRESH ROSEMARY

2 TABLESPOONS PECAN TRUFFLE OIL

1   Preheat the oven to 350 degrees.

2   Season the chicken with salt and pepper on both sides.

3   In a large cast iron skillet, heat the pecan oil over medium heat. Sear the chicken for about 4 minutes per side. Then turn off the heat.

4   In a small bowl combine the garlic, broth, rosemary, and truffle oil, and pour it over the chicken.

5   Place the chicken in the oven for 30 minutes or until cooked through. Serve hot.

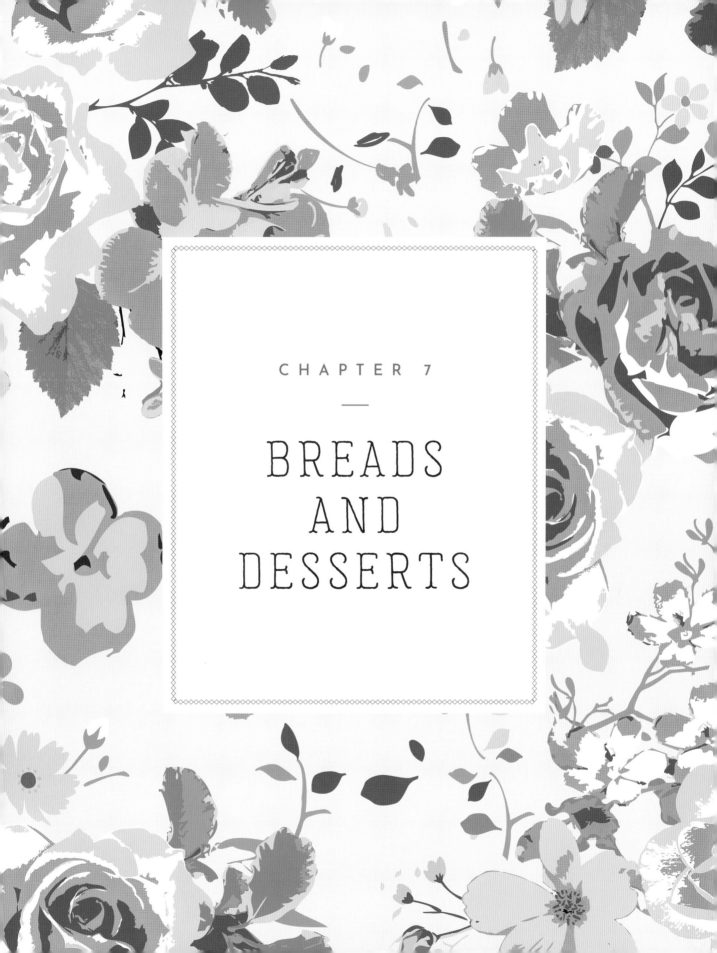

CHAPTER 7

—

BREADS AND DESSERTS

CHOCOLATE ALMOND ESPRESSO CAKE

Three of my favorite flavors coming together in a coffeecake too good to be reserved just for breakfast!

SERVES 12

2 CUPS ALMOND FLOUR

1/2 TEASPOON BAKING SODA

1 TEASPOON FINE SEA SALT

2 TABLESPOONS INSTANT ESPRESSO GRANULES

3 EGGS

1/2 CUP HONEY

2 TABLESPOONS MAPLE SYRUP

1/2 CUP DARK CHOCOLATE CHIPS

1 TEASPOON ALMOND EXTRACT

1   Preheat the oven to 325 degrees.

2   In a large bowl, mix the dry ingredients together.

3   Add the wet ingredients to the dry and mix well.

4   Fold in the chocolate chips.

5   Pour into a greased 9x9 baking dish and bake for 30 minutes. Serve topped with Whipped Coconut Cream (see page 136), if desired.

CLASSIC SOUTHERN POUND CAKE

Every Southern lady passes down her grandmother's pound cake recipe to the next generation. My grandmother was famous for hers, and I guarantee you that she made literally hundreds of them. I even have her pan with all of the dings and dents in it— talk about a precious treasure. My pound cake is, of course, altered and lightened, but I think that she would be proud of me and what I am doing.

SERVES 12

1 TABLESPOON BAKING SODA

1 TABLESPOON WHITE VINEGAR

1 1/2 CUPS COCONUT SUGAR

4 OUNCES ALMOND-BASED CREAM CHEESE AT ROOM TEMPERATURE

1 1/2 CUPS GHEE OR ORGANIC BUTTER AT ROOM TEMPERATURE

3 EXTRA LARGE EGGS AT ROOM TEMPERATURE

1 1/2 TEASPOONS ALMOND EXTRACT

1/4 CUP BUTTERMILK

1 CUP GLUTEN-FREE ALL-PURPOSE FLOUR

1/2 CUP ALMOND FLOUR

1   Dissolve the baking soda in the vinegar a small bowl.

2   In a large bowl, cream together the sugar, cream cheese, and butter.

3   Add the eggs one at a time followed by the almond extract. Add the buttermilk and baking soda-vinegar mixture.

4   Mix in the flours 1/2 cup at a time, mixing well after each addition. Pour the mixture into a greased and wax paper-lined loaf pan.

5   Place the pan in a cold oven. Turn the oven on to 350 degrees and bake for 55-60 minutes.

6   Remove the cake from the oven and allow it to cool in the pan for 15 minutes.

7   Carefully remove it from the pan and remove the paper from the bottom of the loaf. Cool the cake on a wire rack.

COCONUT LIME CAKE

This cake is a party on a plate and my favorite to serve with a Mexican-themed dinner!

1 1/2 CUPS ALMOND FLOUR

1/2 CUP COCONUT FLOUR

1/2 CUP COCONUT FLAKES, UNSWEETENED

1/2 TEASPOON BAKING SODA

1 TEASPOON FINE SEA SALT

2 TABLESPOONS LIME ZEST

3 EGGS

1/2 CUP HONEY

2 TABLESPOONS LIME JUICE

1 TEASPOON ALMOND EXTRACT

2 TABLESPOON COCONUT SUGAR

1   Preheat the oven to 325 degrees.

2   In a large bowl, mix together the dry ingredients except for the coconut sugar.

3   Add the wet ingredients to the dry and mix well.

4   Pour into a greased 9x9 baking dish and bake for 30 minutes. Or pour into two round cake pans sprayed and lined with parchment paper.

5   Sprinkle coconut sugar on top. Bake for 18-20 minutes.

6   Cool completely and top with Whipped Coconut Cream (see page 136).

CRANBERRY ORANGE COFFEE CAKE

This recipe is one of my favorites to serve during the holidays. The recipe can easily be turned into muffins or mini loafs to give as gifts at Christmas!

SERVES 12

2 CUPS ALMOND FLOUR

1/2 TEASPOON BAKING SODA

1 TEASPOON FINE SEA SALT

ZEST OF 2 ORANGES

3 EGGS

1/2 CUP HONEY

2 TABLESPOONS MAPLE SYRUP

2 TABLESPOONS COCONUT OIL

2 TABLESPOONS FRESH ORANGE JUICE

1 TEASPOON VANILLA EXTRACT

1/2 CUP DRIED CRANBERRIES

1 TABLESPOON COCONUT SUGAR

1   Preheat the oven to 325 degrees.

2   In a large bowl, mix dry ingredients together except for the coconut sugar.

3   Add the wet ingredients to the dry and mix well.

4   Fold in the dried cranberries.

5   Pour in a greased 9x9 baking pan and sprinkle the top with the coconut sugar.

6   Bake for 30 minutes and allow to cool before serving.

HONEY CORNBREAD

Life without cornbread? Never! I love the little touch of sweet in this recipe.

2 CUPS GLUTEN-FREE CORNMEAL

1/4 CUP COCONUT SUGAR

1/2 TEASPOON FINE SEA SALT

1/2 TEASPOON BAKING SODA

2 EGGS

1/4 CUP PECAN OIL

1 CUP MILK OR ALMOND MILK

1/3 CUP HONEY

1   Preheat the oven to 400 degrees.

2   Mix all the ingredients together and pour into a greased cast iron skillet.

3   Bake for 15-20 minutes.

LEMON BLUEBERRY MUFFINS

Blueberry muffins are always a hit. I love to make a double batch and freeze half to have on hand for busy weekday morning breakfasts!

SERVES 12

2 CUPS ALMOND FLOUR

1/2 TEASPOON BAKING SODA

1 TEASPOON FINE SEA SALT

ZEST OF 2 LEMONS

3 EGGS

1/2 CUP HONEY

2 TABLESPOONS LEMON JUICE

1 TEASPOON VANILLA EXTRACT

2 TABLESPOONS COCONUT SUGAR

1 CUP FRESH BLUEBERRIES

1   Preheat the oven to 350 degrees.

2   In a large bowl, mix the dry ingredients together except for the coconut sugar.

3   Add the wet ingredients and the coconut sugar to the dry ingredients and mix well.

4   Gently fold in the blueberries; be careful not to overmix.

5   Pour into lined muffin tins and bake for about 20 minutes.

PEAR CRISP

When you want to "taste" fall, make this Pear Crisp. All of the flavors you think of when you think of fall come together in this comfort food dessert.

SERVES 12

TOPPING

1 1/2 CUPS ALMOND FLOUR

1/2 CUP COCONUT FLOUR

1 CUP COCONUT SUGAR

1 CUP BUTTER MELTED

1   Preheat oven to 400 degrees.

2   In a large bowl, mix together the almond flour, coconut flour, coconut sugar, and butter. Set aside.

CRISP

2 TABLESPOONS COCONUT OIL

1 CUP COCONUT SUGAR

1/2 TEASPOON NUTMEG

1 TEASPOON CINNAMON

1/2 TEASPOON GROUND CLOVES

8 BARTLETT PEARS, CORED AND SLICED

1/2 CUP CHOPPED WALNUTS

1   In a small bowl, whisk together the coconut oil, coconut sugar, nutmeg, cinnamon, and clove.

2   Toss the pears and walnuts together with the sugar and spice mixture to coat the fruit well.

3   Pour the fruit into a 9x13 baking dish and sprinkle the topping evenly over the fruit.

4   Bake for 35–40 minutes.

COCONUT CUSTARD

I love serving individual desserts at small dinner parties. Pretty little ramekins centered on a dessert plate, sprinkled with a little toasted coconut on the plate, as well as the whipped coconut cream makes a beautiful presentation for this custard.

SERVES 6

1 1/2 CUPS COCONUT MILK

1 CUP COCONUT SUGAR

3/4 CUP UNSWEETENED SHREDDED COCONUT

2 LARGE EGGS, BEATEN

3 TABLESPOONS COCONUT FLOUR

1/4 TEASPOON VANILLA EXTRACT

1/4 TEASPOON ALMOND EXTRACT

1   Preheat the oven to 400 degrees.

2   In a large bowl, mix all ingredients together and pour into 6 ramekins that have been sprayed with cooking spray.

3   Place the ramekins on a baking sheet and bake for about 25 minutes or until set.

4   Cool completely and top with Whipped Coconut Cream (see page 136).

PECAN BRITTLE

My favorite "candy" in the world is pecan brittle. This one definitely satisfies my sweet tooth!

3/4 CUP HONEY

1/4 CUP WATER

1 CUP CHOPPED PECANS

1 TABLESPOON GHEE (OR BUTTER)

1 TEASPOON PURE VANILLA EXTRACT

1 TEASPOON BAKING SODA

1   Boil the honey and water together until it reaches 235 degrees.

2   Add the pecans and cook for 3 more minutes, stirring constantly.

3   Remove the pan from the heat and stir in the ghee, vanilla, and baking soda.

4   Pour the mixture on a parchment-lined baking sheet and allow it to cool completely.

5   Break it apart and enjoy.

CHRISTMAS CANDY BARK

This is the perfect holiday treat to get the kids involved. You handle the chocolate and let them handle the decorating!

SERVES 6

1 12-OUNCE BAG 60 PERCENT DARK
 CHOCOLATE COCOA CHIPS

1 TABLESPOON COCONUT OIL

1 CUP UNSWEETENED DRIED CRANBERRIES

ZEST OF ONE ORANGE

1   Melt the chocolate with the coconut oil in a bowl over a pot of simmering water. Stir frequently while the chocolate melts.

2   Once the mixture is completely melted, pour it on a parchment-lined baking sheet and spread to 1/8 inch thickness.

3   Sprinkle the melted chocolate with the cranberries and orange zest.

4   Place the chocolate in the refrigerator for 30 minutes.

5   Remove the chocolate from the refrigerator and break into large pieces.

PUMPKIN FUDGE

I like to serve the pumpkin fudge in little balls at a party that people can eat in one bite. I will "dust" the plate with fresh nutmeg for serving!

SERVES 8

2 CUPS ALMOND BUTTER

1/3 CUP COCONUT OIL

1/2 CUP PUMPKIN PUREE

1/4 CUP MAPLE SYRUP

2 TABLESPOONS COCONUT SUGAR

1/2 TEASPOON GROUND CINNAMON

1/2 TEASPOON GROUND NUTMEG

1/2 TEASPOON GROUND CLOVE

1   Line an 8x8 baking dish with parchment paper.

2   In a saucepan, melt the almond butter and coconut oil together over low heat.

3   Stir in the remaining ingredients and mix well.

4   Pour the mixture into the lined baking dish and refrigerate until firm. Store in the refrigerator.

PUMPKIN STREUSEL COFFEE CAKE

This is what Saturday mornings are made for! Pour a second cup of coffee, and enjoy a slice of this moist and delicious coffeecake!

SERVES 12

TOPPING

1/4 CUP COCONUT FLOUR

1/2 CUP ALMOND FLOUR

2 TABLESPOONS COCONUT SUGAR

1/2 TEASPOON CINNAMON

1/2 TEASPOON CLOVE

1/2 TEASPOON NUTMEG

3 TABLESPOONS MAPLE SYRUP

1 TABLESPOON COCONUT OIL

CAKE

1/4 CUP COCONUT OIL, MELTED

1/4 CUP MAPLE SYRUP

1/4 CUP COCONUT SUGAR

1 CUP PUMPKIN PUREE

4 EGGS AT ROOM TEMPERATURE

1/4 CUP COCONUT FLOUR

1 CUP ALMOND FLOUR

1/2 CUP CHOPPED PECANS OR WALNUTS

1/2 TEASPOON BAKING SODA

1 TEASPOON CINNAMON

1/2 TEASPOON CLOVE

1/2 TEASPOON NUTMEG

1/2 TEASPOON SALT

1   Preheat the oven to 325 degrees.

2   To make the crumb topping, combine all the topping ingredients in a bowl and stir well with a fork. Set aside.

3   To make the cake, in a large mixing bowl, combine the wet ingredients together and mix well.

4   Slowly add the dry ingredients and mix well.

5   Pour into a 9x9 greased baking dish, put the topping on, and bake for 45 minutes.

WHIPPED COCONUT CREAM

A scoop of this sweet whipped cream is the perfect topping for desserts . . . or just licking straight from the bowl!

SERVES 6

1 CAN (14 OUNCES) OF FULL-FAT COCONUT
  MILK, CHILLED IN REFRIGERATOR OVERNIGHT
1 TEASPOON VANILLA EXTRACT (OR ALMOND
EXTRACT)
1 1/2 TABLESPOONS MAPLE SYRUP (OR HONEY)

1   Open the can of coconut milk. When it is cold, the fat solids will rise to the top. Remove the solid part from the can.

2   Whip the coconut milk solids, extract. and syrup together.

3   Store in the refrigerator.

CHAPTER 8

KIDS IN THE KITCHEN

APPLE RING PIZZAS

Kids can let their creativity flow and have a delicious time making these "pizzas"!

SERVES 12

3 APPLES, CORED AND SLICED IN RINGS

1/4 CUP PEANUT BUTTER

1/4 CUP HONEY

2 TABLESPOONS ORGANIC DARK CHOCOLATE CHIPS, CHOPPED FINE

2 TABLESPOONS UNSALTED PEANUTS, CHOPPED FINE

1   Arrange apple slices on a tray.

2   In a small bowl, stir together the peanut butter and honey.

3   Drizzle the mixture over the apple slices.

4   Sprinkle the chocolate chips and peanuts over the apples and serve.

CHUNKY MONKEY TRAIL MIX

This is one of my favorite recipes to bag up and share at preschool parties!

SERVES 12

3 TABLESPOONS COCONUT OIL	1 CUP COCONUT FLAKES, UNSWEETENED
1/2 CUP COCONUT SUGAR	1 TEASPOON VANILLA EXTRACT
1 1/2 CUPS PECANS	1 CUP ORGANIC DARK CHOCOLATE CHIPS
1 CUP CASHEWS	2 CUPS BANANA CHIPS, UNSWEETENED

1   Mix the first four ingredients together in a slow cooker and cook the mixture on high for 45 minutes, stirring every 15 minutes.

2   Turn off the slow cooker and stir in the remaining ingredients until the chocolate is melted.

3   Pour the mixture onto a pan lined with parchment paper and allow it to cool completely.

4   Break the cooled mixture up into bite-size pieces and store in an airtight container.

DYLAN'S FAVORITE CHOCOLATE CHIP COOKIES

Is there anything better than a cookie warm from the oven? My little Dylan loves to make these to share with his big brothers!

SERVES 18

4 TABLESPOONS ORGANIC BUTTER AT ROOM TEMPERATURE

1/4 CUP COCONUT OIL

3/4 CUP COCONUT SUGAR

2 TABLESPOONS MAPLE SYRUP

2 TEASPOONS PURE VANILLA EXTRACT

2 EGGS AT ROOM TEMPERATURE

3 CUPS ALMOND FLOUR

1/2 TEASPOON BAKING SODA

1/2 TEASPOON FINE SEA SALT

1 CUP ORGANIC DARK CHOCOLATE CHIPS

1/2 CUP CHOPPED PECANS

1   Preheat the oven to 350 degrees and line a stoneware baking pan with parchment paper.

2   In a large bowl, beat the butter, coconut oil, coconut sugar, syrup, vanilla, and eggs together.

3   In a separate bowl, combine the almond flour, soda, and salt together.

4   Add the dry mixture to the wet ingredients 1/2 cup at a time. Stir in the chocolate chips and nuts.

5   Place the dough on the parchment paper using a melon ball scoop to keep the cookies even in size.

6   Bake 12–13 minutes.

7   Cool and enjoy. You can also freeze these cookies and take out just a few at a time!

KEY LIME PIE POPSICLES

Cool and refreshing! These make a perfect treat for hot summer days!

6 TABLESPOONS GLUTEN-FREE GRAHAM CRACKERS, CRUSHED

8 OUNCES GREEK OR ALMOND-BASED KEY LIME YOGURT

1 CUP COCONUT MILK

2 TABLESPOONS KEY LIME JUICE

2 TABLESPOONS MAPLE SYRUP

1   Divide the cracker crumbs evenly among 6 popsicle containers.

2   Mix the other ingredients together and pour evenly among the popsicle containers.

3   Freeze and enjoy!

PECAN CREAM PIE POPSICLES

A pop with the added nutrition of pecan meal? Go ahead and indulge!

SERVES 6

1/4 CUP MAPLE SYRUP

1/4 CUP FINELY CHOPPED PECANS

1 CUP COCONUT MILK

1 TEASPOON VANILLA EXTRACT

8 OUNCES KITE HILL CREAM CHEESE (OR OTHER PLANT-BASED CREAM CHEESE)

1   Whip all ingredients together in a blender and divide evenly among eight popsicle containers.

1   Freeze and enjoy!

PEANUT BUTTER CUPS

These candies make great Christmas gifts for neighbors and friends. Keep several candy bags on hand to take out the door for a sweet little Christmas treat.

SERVES 8

9 OUNCES OF ORGANIC DARK CHOCOLATE CHIPS

1/3 CUP NATURAL PEANUT BUTTER

1/3 CUP PECAN MEAL

1   Melt the chocolate chips in a double boiler over simmering water. Remove the chocolate from the heat.

2   Stir in the peanut butter first and then the pecan meal.

3   Pour the chocolate by tablespoons into greased mini muffin tins and chill.

4   Once the mixture is set, use a butter knife to help to pop them out of the tin.

5   Keep them in the refrigerator until you are ready to serve.

PEPPERMINT PATTIES

Santa will love having these minty treats left out for him on Christmas Eve!

SERVES 8

9 OUNCES ORGANIC DARK CHOCOLATE CHIPS   2 TABLESPOONS PURE PEPPERMINT EXTRACT

2 TABLESPOONS COCONUT OIL

1   Melt the chocolate in a double boiler over simmering water. Remove the chocolate from the heat.

2   Stir in the coconut oil first and then the peppermint.

3   Pour the chocolate by tablespoons into greased mini muffin tins and chill.

4   Once the mixture is set, use a butter knife to help to pop them out of the tin.

5   Keep them in the refrigerator until you are ready to serve.

PINEAPPLE MANGO WHIP

This tropical treat is super refreshing. For a festive presentation, hollow out a pineapple to use as a bowl!

2 CUPS PINEAPPLE, FROZEN

2 CUPS MANGO, FROZEN

1 TABLESPOON LIME JUICE

1 CUP OF ALMOND MILK

1   Combine all ingredients in a blender and serve.

TRAIL MIX

I love to make up several batches of this trail mix and divide it up into little Halloween treat bags as an alternative to candy for trick-or-treaters!

SERVES 6

1/2 CUP PUMPKIN SEEDS

1 CUP PECANS

1 TABLESPOON COCONUT OIL, MELTED

1 TEASPOON CINNAMON

1/2 TEASPOON COARSE SALT

1/2 CUP DRIED CRANBERRIES

1/2 CUP ORGANIC DARK CHOCOLATE CHIPS

1   Preheat the oven to 400 degrees.

2   Toss the pumpkin seeds, pecans, and oil together in a bowl to coat the nuts.

3   Spread the pecan mixture on a baking sheet and toast in the oven for 6–7 minutes.

4   Remove the nuts from the oven and sprinkle with the cinnamon and salt.

5   Allow the mixture to cool completely. Once cool, toss the cranberries and chocolate chips in.

6   Store in an airtight container.

WATERMELON SKEWERS

with Lime Drizzle

As if watermelon could be any more delicious on a hot summer day! These handheld treats are perfect for cookouts and beach picnics!

SERVES 10

1 LARGE WATERMELON

4 OUNCES PLANT-BASED CREAM CHEESE

4 OUNCES PLANT-BASED KEY LIME YOGURT

2 TABLESPOONS FRESH LIME JUICE

ZEST FROM 1 LIME

2 TABLESPOONS HONEY

1   Cut the watermelon into large strips or "skewers" that kids can hold without a wooden skewer.

2   Arrange the watermelon skewers on a tray. Mix the remaining ingredients together and drizzle over the skewers.

CHAPTER 9

—

DRINKS

CRANBERRY APPLE CIDER

Fill a crockpot with this cider so that family and friends can help themselves. This is also the perfect drink to fill a thermos with for a chilly football game.

SERVES 10

3 LITERS PURE APPLE CIDER

1 LITER PURE CRANBERRY JUICE (NOT JUICE COCKTAIL)

2 CUPS COCONUT SUGAR

6 CINNAMON STICKS

12 CLOVES

1   Mix all ingredients together and simmer for 45 minutes to 1 hour before serving.

CHAI LATTE

SERVES 4

4 CUPS WATER

8 CHAI TEA BAGS

2/3 CUP COCONUT SUGAR

4 CUPS ALMOND MILK

1 Fill a teapot with 4 cups of water and brew the 8 tea bags.

2 Allow the tea to steep for 20 minutes. Discard the tea bags.

3 Dissolve the coconut sugar in the warm tea.

4 If planning to serve cold, chill the mixture and combine with the almond milk.

5 If serving hot, pour the tea mixture and the almond milk into a large pot and heat over low-medium heat until warm.

ESPRESSO SMOOTHIE

My Espresso Smoothie would be the drink of envy at any coffee shop!

◇◇◇

SERVES 2

8 OUNCES UNSWEETENED VANILLA-FLAVORED ALMOND MILK

2 1/2 TEASPOONS INSTANT ESPRESSO POWDER

1 BANANA, PEELED AND FROZEN

1 CONTAINER (5 OUNCES) ALMOND-BASED VANILLA YOGURT

2 TEASPOONS MAPLE SYRUP

1/2 TEASPOON GROUND CINNAMON

1   Combine all ingredients in a blender and serve.

HOT SPICED TEA

This tea is from my childhood. My mother would make this in the winter, and the whole house would smell amazing. This is perfect for a Christmas party.

⬥⬥⬥

SERVES 8

4 CUPS WATER

3 FAMILY-SIZE TEA BAGS

3 CINNAMON STICKS

8 CLOVES

JUICE OF 2 ORANGES

JUICE OF 1 LEMON

HONEY OR STEVIA

1   In a pot, combine the water, tea bags, cinnamon sticks, and cloves together.

2   Bring the mixture to a boil then remove from heat and cover. Allow the tea to steep for 30 minutes.

3   Strain the tea into a pitcher and discard the spices.

4   Add the orange and lemon juices and stir. Add honey or stevia to taste. Serve warm.

5   This will keep in a pitcher in the refrigerator for 3-4 days.

BANANA NUT SMOOTHIE

My favorite breakfast bread was the inspiration for this smoothie. Not only is the smoothie delicious, but the pecan meal provides healthy nutrition and a rich flavor.

SERVES 2

2 CUPS ALMOND MILK

2 BANANAS, FROZEN

1/2 CUP PECAN MEAL

1/4 CUP MAPLE SYRUP (OR HONEY)

1/2 TEASPOON CINNAMON

1/2 CUP VANILLA ALMOND YOGURT

1/4 TEASPOON GRATED FRESH NUTMEG

1 Combine all ingredients in a blender.

PUMPKIN SPICE LATTE

Let the leaves fall and the crisp air blow! This recipe is my favorite fall drink, and it packs a nutritional punch with the pumpkin!

SERVES 4

1 CUP ALMOND MILK

2 TABLESPOONS PUMPKIN PUREE

1 TABLESPOON MAPLE SYRUP

1/4 TEASPOON VANILLA EXTRACT

1/8 TEASPOON CINNAMON

1/8 TEASPOON NUTMEG

1/8 TEASPOON CLOVE

1/4 CUP STRONG COFFEE

1   Combine all ingredients together and warm over low-medium heat.

ROSEMARY TEA

There is nothing better than sitting on a porch swing and sipping a glass of sweet tea.

2 FAMILY-SIZE DECAFFEINATED BLACK TEA BAGS

8 CUPS WATER

2 DECAFFEINATED EARL GREY TEA BAGS

2 6-INCH SPRIGS FRESH ROSEMARY

1 CUP HONEY OR STEVIA

1   Bring the tea bags to a boil in the water. Remove from heat.

2   Add rosemary and allow the tea to steep for 1 hour.

3   Discard the tea bags and pour the tea mixture into a gallon pitcher.

4   Add your sweetener and stir well.

5   Fill the rest of the pitcher with water and chill before serving.

SUNRISE SMOOTHIE

Beau is my "smoothie expert" and this is one of his favorites!

SERVES 4

2 BANANAS, FROZEN

1/2 CUP FROZEN PINEAPPLE

1/2 CUP ORANGE JUICE

1/2 CUP LIGHT COCONUT MILK

1 TEASPOON PURE VANILLA EXTRACT

1   Mix all ingredients together in a blender and serve.

ABOUT THE AUTHOR

Lara Lyn Carter won her first Emmy in the category of On-Camera Talent for hosting *Thyme for Sharing with Lara Lyn Carter,* which she also created and produced. It aired in June 2015 as part of Georgia Public Broadcasting's summer cooking lineup and received excellent ratings and praise. The show was nominated for four Emmys in the categories of lighting, photography, directing, and on-camera talent. In addition, Lara Lyn created and hosted *Savor the Good Life* with Raycom Media's WALB, the NBC and ABC affiliate in Southwest Georgia, for three years. This show received a GABBY (Georgia Association of Broadcasters) Award in its first year. She has also appeared on the Food Network show, *The Kitchen.*

Lara Lyn is considered Georgia's go-to authority on Southern entertaining, adding her healthy, clean-cooking twist. Lara shares her vast experience and array of Southern recipes with her constantly growing followers. She has been featured in numerous magazines, newspapers, and radio shows across the US and Canada.

As both a television and private chef, Lara Lyn has entertained and cooked for people from coast to coast and at numerous food and wine festivals, including the Telluride Wine and Food Festival in Colorado and the Food Network South Beach Wine and Food Festival in Miami. Lara Lyn is also the brand ambassador for Polo in the Pines, an organization that raises money for pediatric brain cancer research.

Lara Lyn completed a major media tour in Canada in January 2017 for national media including television, radio, and filming live with Yahoo! and Diply. She showed the Canadians her true Southern hospitality.

When not working, Lara Lyn keeps herself busy with her husband and their three sons, ages twenty-two, sixteen, and five.

ABOUT FAMILIUS

Familius is a book publisher dedicated to helping families be happy. We believe that the family is the fundamental unit of society and that happy families are the foundation of a happy life. The greatest work anyone will ever do will be within the walls of his or her own home. And we don't mean vacuuming! We recognize that every family looks different and passionately believe in helping all families find greater joy, whatever their situation. To that end, we publish beautiful books that help families live our 9 Habits of Happy Family Life:

- Love Together
- Play Together
- Learn Together
- Work Together
- Talk Together
- Heal Together
- Read Together
- Eat Together
- Laugh Together

Website: www.familius.com
Facebook: www.facebook.com/paterfamilius
Twitter: @familiustalk, @paterfamilius1
Pinterest: www.pinterest.com/familius

The most important work you ever do will be within the walls of your own home.

CONVERSIONS

VOLUME MEASUREMENTS

U.S.	METRIC
1 teaspoon	5 ml
1 tablespoon	15 ml
1/4 cup	60 ml
1/3 cup	75 ml
1/2 cup	125 ml
2/3 cup	150 ml
3/4 cup	175 ml
1 cup	250 ml

WEIGHT MEASUREMENTS

U.S.	METRIC
1/2 ounce	15 g
1 ounce	30 g
3 ounces	90g
4 ounces	115 g
8 ounces	225 g
12 ounces	350 g
1 pound	450 g
2 1/4 pounds	1 kg

TEMPERATURE CONVERSION

FAHRENHEIT	CELSIUS
250	120
300	150
325	160
350	180
375	190
400	200
425	220
450	230